WINNING TRUTHS

The book on whatever you're into

KEVIN ABDULRAHMAN

JAICO PUBLISHING HOUSE

Ahmedabad Bangalore Bhopal Bhubaneswar Chennai
Delhi Hyderabad Kolkata Lucknow Mumbai

Published by Jaico Publishing House
A-2 Jash Chambers, 7-A Sir Phirozshah Mehta Road
Fort, Mumbai - 400 001
jaicopub@jaicobooks.com
www.jaicobooks.com

WINNING TRUTHS
ISBN 978-81-8495-190-5

First Jaico Impression: 2011
Reissued: 2013
Originally published as *The Book on Whatever You're Into*

Printed by
Repro India Limited
Plot No. 50/2, T.T.C. MIDC Industrial Area
Mahape, Navi Mumbai - 400 710.

What the World has to say about Kevin Abdulrahman's Book

"Only a few people really understand that success starts with your inner world. Kevin focuses on your inner world, more specifically your mind. An insightful and empowering book to help unlock your true potential and live the life of a winner."

Jay Conrad Levinson, The Father Author of "Guerrilla Marketing" series of books and best known marketing brand in history. Named one of the 100 best business books ever written. Over 20 million sold; now in 62 languages. www.gmbu.com — Guerrilla Marketing Business University.

"Kevin has a knack for presenting simple, direct and timeless truths about success. *'Whatever You're Into'* is one-year game plan for staying focused, inspired and moving toward your dreams."

Randy Gage, Author Prosperity Mind, www.RandyGage.com

"Kevin's book, *Whatever Your Into,* touches 52 points that touch on the forces behind success. After you read this empowering book, you shall see that you do have the power to achieve."

Thomas J. Senatore, Tax Lien and Tax Deed Expert, CEO — TLD International.

Kevin Abdulrahman puts life in the palm of your hand and challenges you to celebrate the struggle.

Mrs Tania (Nee Matejcic) Bruss, Zimbabwe

"I have faced several traumatic life's experiences, most of the challenges created myself to be positive thinking and this book gives me an insight of my winning streak in Life — It has made me a successful person again!"

Quintus Pillai, Vice President Sales & Marketing, ISCS, Sharjah, UAE

"Kevin Abdulrahman is truly an inspiration." *Whatever You're Into* "is a recipe book for success. A must read for anyone looking to succeed in life."

Emma Quintin, Actress/Presenter, UK — www.emmaquintin.com

"Once again, Kevin has crafted a very useful book in his trademark succinct style. With 52 lessons there is one to follow each week of the year. A very good guide to practice."

David Payne, Networker & Life Adventurer — http://davidrpayne.wordpress.com

This book ticks all the boxes and is recommended for anyone wanting to bring out the best in themselves.

Brendan O Shea, CEO, Chamber Group

"*Whatever You're Into* is a must read book for anyone who wants to bring the best out of them."

Mukhtar Aidarus, Property Investment Advisor, Canada

"Kevin Abdulrahman's teachings are an indispensable guide to excel and win, *Whatever You're Into*."

Claire R. Kanj, Creative Director, www.size-34.com

"THE BOOK on *Whatever You're Into* adds the EXTRA into Ordinary. A sneak peek into the world called Success with simple yet stunning truths for anyone wanting to become a winner."

Nitin Mirani, Actor & International Standup Comedian, www.nitinmirani.com, India

"My favorite 'Ebyism' is 'Change is a door that can only be opened from the inside!'

Success is an inside job! Kevin's book focuses on your inner world, particularly your mind. 'YOUR' world is in 'YOUR' mind! Change your mind ... change your world. This book will help you do that!"

Gary Eby, Speaker, TV Personality and Author of "Left Handed Soldiers" Published by Jim Roh N International at: www.freebook.tv

"Kevin tears away the clutter and mystery of what makes some succeed while others fail. Read this book if you are ready to go to the next level in your life's success story."

Guy Whitcroft, CEO, Dubai

"A great no-nonsense introduction to achieving your goals and creating a successful life for yourself."

Ananda Shakespeare, Journalist and Entrepreneur — UK

"It doesn't matter who you are, where you are from or what you did. This book can instantly change your life."

Paritosh Palav, Managing Editor/General Manager, Maxmedia Company WLL, Bahrain

"Kevin believes that life is a game. You have to play, fail, play, fail and play again. What he teaches will help you play smarter until you get to the summit of your choice."

Sami Dababneh, Assitant HR Manager, Arabtec

"Comprehensive in the way it's written, Powerful in its message. If you were to read three books this year, make sure Kevin's book *Whatever You're Into* is one of them."

Michael A. Aun, FIC, LUTCF, CSP, CPAE Speaker Hall of Fame — www.aunline.com

"I have found *Whatever You're Into* to be very insightful, interesting and on-target motivating. The 52 winning truths presented formulate a well balanced winning formula and I feel eager to personally start consciously living them as Kevin suggests."

Zunaira Munir Ph.D., Managing Director. Affiliate Member of the Blue Ocean Strategy Network, San Diego — www.strategizeblue.com

Are you really, really serious about becoming a winner? Can you handle the truth? If you answered "Yes" to both questions, Kevin's book is a must for you to read! Rarely does someone tell you the real truth and that is exactly what Kevin does!

Scott Letourneau, CEO www.FastBusinessCredit.com and www.FastBusinessStartUp.com

Everyone has or has been challenged with what separates winners from the rest. Kevin gives immediate insights on how winners operate in their life.

Mr Renit Shah, Entrepreneur, London, UK.

"Kevin Abdulrahman's teachings is an indispensable guide to excel and win whatever you're into. In my personal life, I saw many things as complicated, after reading 'uncomplicate the complicated' (Winning Truth # 3) I have a different perspective and I'm able to get over some of my 'mental blocks'."

Naeem M Sufi, President, Sufi Group USA, Inc. — www.mallroad247.com

If you value your life and want to save years, then I would recommend you listen to what Kevin has to say. Invaluable and timeless winning truths are shared that is all too often missed by many.

Roxana Chegin, Born Artist, Producer, Singer, Presenter — www.persianwave.com

This chap is a go-getter — and he wants you to be one too. A lot of home-truths that we forget about, and positive thinking techniques to help you remember them again. I like his style of homely anecdotes that everyone can relate to.

Linda Benbow, Editor, UAE Digest and Dubai Real Times

If you don't strive to be great, then you will be surpassed. Whether you are financially set, successful in your line of work, an achiever in your own right, a winner in sport or happy with your life all together, there is still room for you to grow. Kevin Abdulrahman's book will help push you to what he refers to as the Next Level.

Reza Naderi, Artist and Teacher — www.RezaNaderi.com

Dedication

This book has come about from people wondering what aspects of their lives is Mind Nutrition important for.

The answer is in your hands………… *Whatever You're Into*.

Contents

Preface

If you are reading this book, then it means that you have taken the first step in investing in yourself. Congratulations! You value yourself. I respect and admire anyone who takes pride in constantly nourishing their mind.

I hope that you take the time to go over this book that I have put together. It's not complicated, the layout is simple, and I have stayed clear from creating any bog down areas. I wanted it to be an easy read because the power of each truth is enormous. I ensured every truth was wrapped up and to the point, giving you quality over quantity.

Don't be fooled by its simplicity. After all, one simple truth alone could unlock your potential to create better results in both your personal and professional life. One small change in your life will make your return on investment infinite.

I know some of you are thinking, 'Will this book help me succeed? Is this all I'll ever need?'

Yes and no.

Yes because you will learn Powerful Timeless Winning Truths.

No, because you should never stop learning (something you will be reminded of in this book). The book, in its own entirety is purely a tool to make you aware. It's then up to you to implement these truths and turn around winning results.

If you have the heart and the courage then you can take what you learn in this book and become a winner.

As I share with you each truth, I ask you to take the time to stop after every chapter. Take the time to chew on the info, analyze it, and then practice making it a part of you, as any winner would.

After all, these are the Timeless Winning Truths lived by those who are winning. Not just in terms of finances, or record breaking achievements, but those who are mentally and emotionally in a day to day *winning* state, where they live everyday doing what they love, being massively rewarded for it, and most important of all, they are happy

... something that is easily said, but sadly, is rarely seen in the lives of the majority.

Some of you will choose to read the entire book in one sitting. That works fine.

In fact read through the book the first time to get a feel for things.

Then come back and read the first timeless truth and really work on consciously applying it in your life in the first week. Apply one timeless truth at a time in every subsequent week. I believe that doing so would be the best. After all, days will go by, weeks will go by and soon, yet another year will escape us all. By consciously ensuring you ingrain each truth and committing to really work and make the relevant truth part of each week, you will come out a winner at the end of the year.

This will also avoid your feeling of being overwhelmed with too much information which leads to many never ever making a serious change. The journey of a thousand miles starts with the first step, and by applying one truth a week, you will become a completely different person by the end of 52 weeks.

Some of you might say that's too long, then that's fine, you can do it in days, or hours.

I will leave that choice to be yours.

Here's a warning in advance.

You will find me to be blunt in some instances if I feel it's of importance to drive my message home to you. So take my words to heart with the understanding that I have your best interest in mind.

My intention is to help you become better, expand further, create breakthrough results, and reach for the Next Level in your life whether it's personally or professionally, or ideally both.

... So let's get started

Winning Truth Number

1

You Have to Die to Go to Heaven

The first four words sound morbid, but the rest of it is what most people hope to achieve (those who believe in higher powers).

That's exactly what winners understand and do (the morbid part) in order to achieve their goals (heaven).

Everyone wants to have nice things in life. They want to travel, excel in their field, break world records, give back to society, create great relationships, have the time and freedom in life, own a successful business and so on, yet not many will do the hard work to get there.

Winners understand that for each of their goal, there is a route that needs to be traveled.

Winners choose the goals that matter to them the most and commit to making that journey. Most people will think that it would be tough, rough and hard to do. However winners know that they are simply going through a process, one that will lead them to heaven so to speak.

I believe that you are well on your way to applying this first truth already.

The fact that you purchased this book and are reading it shows me that you are different. It shows that you are committed.

I say it because just as in life, there would have been many who had the opportunity to pick up this book, wanting to know the truths about why winners win, but were not willing to make the investment money and time, more importantly they were afraid to commit and apply what they would learn.

Whatever goal you may have in place, you must understand and more importantly be prepared to put in the hard yards. Winners are often associated with a 'whatever it takes' attitude, because they will see what they want right through to the end.

They are willing to die in order to go to heaven.

Winners are committed.

Take a moment to reflect on this truth.
Consciously live this truth in week 1.

Winning Truth Number

2

All You Need is a Little Bit

Winners are known for the fact that they will go that extra mile, they will make that extra call, do an extra round on the circuit. Whatever the masses will do, winners always put in that little extra. It doesn't have to be a lot, just a little bit more.

Winners (extraordinary people) are simply ordinary people who do that little extra every time.

Most people have a perception that winners are born great.

Winners aren't born great. They have become great by the virtue of doing a little extra to achieve greatness. That little extra effort accumulates to one day giving them the winning results when compared to the ordinary efforts of others.

It's in the little extra effort that they succeed.

That's the difference of winners who stand out as the champions amongst a sea of players. That's the difference of a low five figure income and a high six figure income. That's the difference in having a good relationship and a great relationship. That's the difference between living in a *wish-world* and actually living your wishes.

As you go along your chosen path, you will come across challenges. Use them as cues to ensure you go that little extra. Every wall you come across, push through harder.

When doubted, double your efforts

When blocked, double your efforts

When talked down to, double your efforts

By using challenges as a positive cue to do a little extra, your efforts will soon be accumulated.

All it takes is just a little bit every time.

Remember it's in that little extra where all winners have realised their breakthrough.

Take a moment to reflect on this truth.
Consciously live this truth in week 2.

Winning Truth Number

3

Uncomplicate the Complicated

How many times have you heard people respond to statements made with, 'oh, it's complicated'?

How many times have you used 'it's complicated' as a reason to justify your actions or inactions?

As humans, it seems to be in our nature to complicate situations. Humans enjoy complicating things to serve their egos. After all we all feel good when we triumph over a complicated situation (you know I'm right).

Life doesn't have to be complicated. But many make it so to justify the time and effort spent in order to get a sense of achievement. When you are afraid, uncertain, or haven't tried something before, you try to complicate things to further justify why you should take your time before making a move. Or even worse, make a move at all.

Winners see things as they are. There are no complications, good or bad.

Everything is simple. Winners are often heard saying, 'it's really simple'.

They are not saying it to make themselves sound superior; they do it because it's their reality.

To them things are really simple.

Winners know that to get what they want; they need to do certain things. They make a decision and get on with the process.

When the majority of people look for a hundred and one reasons to tie knots on a rope, winners will choose to use the rope (and its knots) to their benefit.

Life can be complicated as it is, so why add to it? It makes no sense if you choose to be a winner.

Simply put, winners know that simplicity is power.

Take a moment to reflect on this truth.
Consciously live this truth in week 3.

Winning Truth Number

4

Seek in to Sort Out

So many people are running around life wanting and expecting easy answers to their questions. They are seeking to find solutions from their outer world. What you will find in the outer world is guidance. The solutions are somewhere else. The solutions tend to be right in front of you. The solutions are actually within you.

Winners take responsibility and ownership of their life instead of what is common with the majority of people, constantly moaning and worst yet, blaming others as to why their life is not right. When pointing the finger seems like the easiest way out, winners know that they are 100% responsible for their outcome.

Speaking of pointing the finger, take your index finger and point it at someone. Have you ever thought about how many fingers are actually pointing back your way when you point at someone as the cause of where you are in life? One whole finger points their way and yet four fingers are pointing your way. Follow your fingers because that's where the answers lie.

Why be responsible when you don't have to? Why bother to take ownership? Responsibility and ownership are two words most people shy away from. They are hard enough to digest, and even harder to perform.

Winners know that if they don't, then they will simply be doing what the masses are doing. And if they are doing what the masses are doing, then they are going to get what they have, which is sadly a far cry from a winning result.

Winners have mastered being responsible, because it's the only way to win.

Choose to be responsible for your actions.
Choose to be responsible for what happens.
Choose to be responsible for your life.
Choose to be responsible all the time (not sometimes).

After all, every thing in life is a choice. Choose to be the best you can be. If your life is not where you want it to be, then look into yourself and ask, 'what do I need to do to have the life that I want?'

You are the owner of your life, not anyone else.

Take ownership and understand that much of your life is under your control.

Winners seek in their inner world to sort out their outer world.

Take a moment to reflect on this truth.
Consciously live this truth in week 4.

Winning Truth Number

5

The Confidence to Know

Opportunities are plenty.

I can already hear you scream out, 'what is this guy talking about'? What opportunities? And if there are opportunities, I'm unable to make anything out of it, because this needs a lot of money, which I don't have. This needs time, which I don't have. This needs skills, which I don't have. And if I did, the knowledge required is completely different from my experience and college education.

I'm sure you can think of an array of other reasons why there are no opportunities, or if I was to correct myself, no opportunities that suit you.

Whether it's starting up an online business but not knowing how, making a home based business successful which you've never done, changing careers with no previous experience, or deciding to pick up a sport not having started it as a child, there are plenty of examples out there of people who have been in your position and *still* made it through.

So again, I'll reiterate, opportunities are plenty.

The truth is, it isn't the lack of opportunities you are

facing, more so it's the lack of confidence.

Winners have learned that opportunities are everywhere. Only because there are challenges along the way doesn't mean they won't take up on what is offered. A winner might not be able to play a sport today, yet aspires to play in the Olympics. The winner looks beyond his current abilities and focuses on his desire of being in the Olympics, knowing that the journey there will indeed shape him up to be the person who can compete at that level.

Winners have confidence. They may not have what's needed at the start, but they will most certainly get around it, acquire it, learn it, work it, and do whatever it takes because they know what they want at the end of it. They don't let the reasons be their excuses and *make it happen* in spite of it all.

Have confidence and believe that you will become that capable person needed to reach your goals (which will come from the process of moving towards your goals).

Develop the confidence in knowing so.

Take a moment to reflect on this truth.
Consciously live this truth in week 5.

Winning Truth Number

6

Fuel the Fire

Winners have developed the power and mental strength to ensure any comment made to them fuels their fire. The more comments they hear, the bigger and brighter their fire burns.

They see comments as the firewood that keeps them going.

What type of comments you may ask? Positive and uplifting comments or negative and downright condescending comments?

Well, both.

Winners use positive comments as a pat in the back and further build their confidence to move forward. They also use the negative comments as a boost because now they have so much more to prove. They have to first prove it to themselves that they have what it takes to get what they want. In the process they will also help put the naysayers to shame.

Don't do what most people do. They take negative comments to heart. They use negative comments they hear as reasons to stop doing what they want in life. They let negative comments extinguish their fire.

You are the owner of your life remember? Winners know that the best way to silence their critics is to gain massive results. They don't spend their energy getting into disputes. They rather focus their energy to get results.

So as a winner, learn not to let negative comments affect you. Just treat it as firewood that feeds your fire. Soon that fire will be so big and so bright that those who criticized you will smell the smoke, even if they happen to be on the other side of the world.

Find every way and every reason you can to fuel your fire.

I hope that whilst you are reading and reflecting on this book, I provide you with sufficient fuel in order to get out there and create a winning inferno.

When most people let comments break them, you can now use them to breakthrough.

Get out there and blaze that trail.

Take a moment to reflect on this truth.
Consciously live this truth in week 6.

Winning Truth Number

7

Hello President

I have an announcement to make. Today I would like to officially congratulate you. I want to congratulate you for being the President. Some of you reading this might already be presidents of nations and companies, in which case my best wishes to you are delayed, but for the majority of you reading this, you might ask, 'the President of what'?

In every one of us is a life, waiting to be fully lived. For every life that exists, there is a President that runs it.

You are the President of your life.

You dictate how things go and how you would like to deal with things. This is *your* life. It is your ownership and your responsibility. You are accountable for the good and the bad that's in it. If you want more of the good, and less of the bad, then it is up to you to make that decision and take action.

Like any President, there comes responsibility with your title. You must ensure to utilize the resources around you for maximum good. This means that it will be deemed completely unresourceful of you, to live a life that is far beyond your actual potential. It would be like wasting precious natural resources found within the country, and as a result failing to contribute to society at large.

Do you want to be a President who is remembered or soon forgotten? Those remembered are usually the ones who faced major challenges, more accurately; it's more to do with how they dealt with those challenges.

You have been born with a responsibility, and that's to take your unique talent and ability and create maximum good. Not just for yourself (because that's selfish), but also for the people around you.

Look in the mirror and see the President in you.

There is something that you can do, for a greater good, for a greater cause, one that is far bigger than just yourself.

Find it, and then, do it.

That's what every winner does.

Take a moment to reflect on this truth.
Consciously live this truth in week 7.

Winning Truth Number

8

Only One Category Wins

There are two types of people in this world. Those who will fall in category A, and then there are those, who will fall in Category B.

There are two types of people in this world. Those who fall in the successful minority, and then there are those, who will fall in the majority.

There are two types of people in this world. Those who will point out all the windows in life available, and then there are those, who will always tell you about why life is one big wall.

There are two types of people in this world. Those who will make mistakes and fail repeatedly, and then there are those, who will never do anything in life purely to avoid making a mistake or having to come close to failure.

There are two types of people in this world. Those who will push through *no matter what*, and then there are those who will give up when things get tough.

There are two types of people in this world. Those who will say enough is enough, let's look at the opportunity oasis presented to us now. And then there are those who will only ever enjoy a conversation if it has in it the now two infamous words 'financial crisis'. And if it wasn't for the previous crisis, they would have a list of other so called crisis to talk to you about.

There are two types of people in this world. Those who will attain a Winning Mind, and then there are those, who will be happy with being average living a mediocre life.

We all live in the same world. Most of us have the same access to information. We all have the resources to achieve whatever we choose to achieve, yet two types of people exist. One that will choose to take control and make the most of it (category A), whilst the other who will choose to do nothing (category B).

Which of the two are you?

Winners choose category A when most choose category B. Is it any wonder why most people are often left frustrated, wandering without their desired results?

What will you choose? How will you choose to live your life?

Life is what you make of it. Life is a choice.

Winners merely choose the right category.

Take a moment to reflect on this truth.
Consciously live this truth in week 8.

Winning Truth Number

9

You Don't Have to Be a Genius

Even though there is so much in life that you don't know, you can still enjoy life to it's fullest with what you *do know* whilst continuing to learn everyday.

Winners know that they don't need to know how something works. As long as it works, and they can make the most of it, they will happily use it no questions asked.

Winners know it would be a waste of time trying to figure out why the sun rises from the east and how gravity works (unless that's a field of interest they are studying of course). When most people look for an excuse because they want to know the ins and outs of something, winners push ahead. They know that they don't have to figure everything out to win.

Most of us don't know what electricity really is or how it works. Most of us don't know how a mobile phone actually connects to a network. Most of us don't know how the circuit board in a laptop works? Most of us don't know the exact technicality of being able to listen to music on our iPods. Most of us don't know how the computer really works. Most of us don't know how e-mail, facebook and twitter really works. Most of us don't know how a coffee machine really works. Yet we are competent enough to use and make the most of these products and services to our benefit.

The point is, you don't need to know everything before starting to make a move. If you have a strong *why*, the *how* will follow either by way of knowledge gained through the process, or a partner with that knowledge.

Winners take things that work for what they are without getting bogged down. If something works for everyone else and it can work for you, then use it. It's as simple as that. Make the most of it to serve your purpose.

Winners make decisions and run with what they have. People are often offered opportunities that they let slip because they want to figure it all out before they start.

Don't let that be you.

Seize the opportunity; push the pedal to the metal. The chances are you know more than enough to get you to your destination. And what you don't know, you will learn along the way. You don't have to be a genius to make the most of what is working around you.

**Take a moment to reflect on this truth.
Consciously live this truth in week 9.**

Winning Truth Number

10

K.I.A

Is knowledge power?

If knowledge was power then how come people who are less knowledgeable, less skilled, and even far less talented than you become winners? I'm sure that you have friends who are encyclopedias of information. They can tell you everything about anything. Some have great skills, or are even naturally talented, and yet their results are far short of the knowledge they possess. Generally speaking, why aren't they the winners in life?

I know that you have wondered how? I know that you have wondered why?

After all, you know someone who is far more knowledgeable, far more skilled, and far more talented (yourself of course) that would have been more deserving.

The answer is simple.

Winners get into action and power with what they have rather than mull over things, think it over for generations to come, and over scrutinize a situation as an excuse not to act.

Knowing is not enough. What you have means nothing and winners are smart enough to know that life doesn't reward those with potential. It rewards those who take action.

It's not what you know, but what you do with what you know. It's not what talent or ability you possess, but what you do with what you possess. For the ladies, it's similar to having a beautiful Versace dress and not wearing it. For the gents, imagine having a Lamborghini and not driving it. The term waste comes to mind, and that's exactly what most people do with their lives, waste it.

To know and not do, or to have and not use, is stupidity. Knowledge is not power. The application of knowledge is power.

Winners make moves and put their Knowledge Into Action (K.I.A)

Winners run with what they have. So start running.

Take a moment to reflect on this truth.
Consciously live this truth in week 10.

Winning Truth Number

11

168 Whole Hours in Every Week

Did I just state the obvious?

I can just imagine some of you working out what 24 hours in a day multiplied by 7 days a week is. Yes you have 168 hours in a week. I've triple checked it.

Time is a great equalizer amongst us all, yet winners seem to be able to achieve so much more with their time.

As my friend once put it, subtract 56 hours of sleeping and a couple of hours for being in the bathroom, one has 110 hours that they can control on how to best utilize it.

My intention with this truth is to simply make you aware of your 110 hours.

What is your excuse for why you are not hitting the gym? Starting a business? Expanding your knowledge base? Nurturing your relationships? Networking with people for your success?

There is none.

Winners know there is no excuse. Why?

Because they figure out what's important to them, and make all the time they need for it first. They don't fill their time up with fluff and then say that they are out of time. They block out their time to fit in what's of most importance to them, then work whatever fluff that comes about around it (and by fluff I mean time consuming activities leading nowhere).

Work out where you are spending your 110 hours.

You have 110 whole hours.

Then ask yourself the following questions:

Am I best utilizing my time to reach my goals?

What do I need to spend more time on? What do I need to cut back on?

What am I committed to? If what I am spending my time on is not getting me what I want, how much longer am I going to carry out this insanity?

The answer is simple, and so is the decision to make the best use of 110 hours.

You have now been made aware. There is no excuse.

Take a moment to reflect on this truth. Consciously live this truth in week 11.

Winning Truth Number

12

Winners Are Doers

Have you noticed some people? Every moment they get, they will complain to you about the weather. They will complain about their life, their finances, their kids, their partners, the economy and why it's doom and gloom in the world of business.

These people seem to have developed a habit. They complain!

Most people complain about their life and how it never is where it should be. They tend to be the same people who do nothing about it. What they have mastered, is the art of complaining. You may even have an intimate experience with this.

This habit is far from what a winner would do, want or need. This habit is of absolutely no value to you.

I'm notoriously known to be blunt amongst my circle of friends and clients to say something along the lines of 'Stop complaining and do something about it'. Needless to say I'm not the most loved guy in my circle, but I earn the respect of those who with time come to the true realization of what I mean.

So why do you complain? The reason you complain is because you know what you really can and should be doing, how you really can and should be living, how you really can and should have things, and yet you don't. That is the reason you complain.

A client told me about a realization she had after one of our private executive coaching sessions. She said that when unhappy about any aspect of her life, she decided to 'do something about it'. In the past she would simply complain and do nothing. She finally figured out that she would save herself so much time by simply doing what needs to be done, instead of just grumbling and complaining about it.

Your life is exactly where it should be. If you don't like the result of your past actions, then do something about it. It's in your control. Winners always realize where they are, and where they want to go. Instead of spending hours, days, months and years moaning and complaining, they get on with doing the things that will help them achieve what they desire.

Life favors those who *do*, not those who complain. Winners are doers. If you are unhappy with a situation, then do something about it.

Stop complaining and start doing.

Take a moment to reflect on this truth. Consciously live this truth in week 12.

Winning Truth Number

13

You Better Believe It

Some people are a piece of art. They don't think they're intelligent enough, yet expect others to think otherwise. They don't think they have the goods, yet expect others to think that they do. They don't think they are worth living a full life, yet they expect life to give them an opportunity to do so.

There are hungry people out there who believe that they deserve to live the best of the one life they have. Unless you start believing, you are hitting a brick wall my friend, and this brick wall won't budge until you shift your belief.

Believe in yourself. Believe in your abilities; believe in your talent, your uniqueness on this earth. Believe that there is something in you that's special. Believe that you are here for a reason, that you have something to contribute.

You must believe in *you* before others will do so.

Winners believe that they are winners long before they get their desired results. Roger Federer knew he was a winner long before his 16 Grand Slam titles.

People want to back a winner. They inherently do so

through the vibes they get. The vibes they get are usually from the projection given by those winning. The projections of winners are based on their internal beliefs about themselves.

You are perceived in this world based on the internal beliefs you have of yourself. If you don't believe in you then you can't expect others to do so. You need to hear your belief in your voice and see it in your posture. Belief is what will make you stand out. This belief in yourself will be the lighthouse for others to spot you in a world of 7 billion people.

If your belief about yourself is solid, then keep pushing through. Even if you don't have the support you desire to start off with, sooner or later, others will start believing in you.

In any case, remember that you're a unique individual and most certainly have something to contribute to this world. You better Believe that.

See it in yourself, and the world will follow suit.

Believe in you.

Take a moment to reflect on this truth.
Consciously live this truth in week 13.

Winning Truth Number

14

Everything You Do Has a Price

The price you pay for up-skilling towards a new career means less time in front of the TV. The price you pay to get good grades in your studies is missing out on time spent at the beach. The price of losing weight is the hardship of exercising and good dieting.

This is all common knowledge and many already have a clear understanding of it. In the midst of all the confusion in their minds, most people don't realise that they are paying a hefty price for the actions they don't take. After all inaction in itself is a form of action. Winners are aware and always choose between paying the price for their actions and inactions.

For example, let's choose a goal of losing 9 Kilograms in 3 months.

Winners will on a piece of paper, write down the price they will have to pay to attain their goal. On another piece, they will write the price they'll pay if they don't attain a goal. It will look something like this.

Price to pay to lose 9 Kilograms in 3 months:

Go through the pain of cutting back on eating rice from 14 times to 3 times a week, getting up at 6 am to face cold mornings, disciplined to hit the gym more regularly, less sleep, avoid previous junk food habit.

Price to pay for keeping the 9 Kilograms after 3 months:

Guilt, dissatisfaction when looking in the mirror, low self-confidence, feeling unattractive, sadness, anger, no will-power.

Once they have done so, winners then compare the prices on a mental weighing scale. Which set of prices is heavier? Harder? More painful? What's their life worth? Will taking action or inaction hold them back? Which action will bring them the greatest dissatisfaction in the long term? Which will make them the happiest? Winners choose to make the *smartest sacrifice.*

Become aware of both your actions and inactions. Understand the price you will have to pay in each instance and make a serious decision to do what you need to do. I hope that once you have thought about it long and hard, you will realize that you just can't afford to sit around and do nothing.

You will have to make a sacrifice. Ensure it's a smart and winning one.

**Take a moment to reflect on this truth.
Consciously live this truth in week 14.**

Winning Truth Number

15

Go with Your Gut Feel

Ever experienced that sixth sense feeling? That gut feeling you followed or chose not to follow. Some of you may call it intuition.

The feeling that said, 'yes go for it'. The feeling that said 'be careful of that person'.

Winners have a realization and understanding of going with their gut feel. If the feeling says, 'give it a go', then that's exactly what they do.

In life, you will face the dilemma of going with your head, or going with what your gut feel tells you to do. In my experience, going with my gut feel has helped in many instances. If you have a feeling of doing something (and there are a thousand things that prove your feeling otherwise), stick to your guns.

Winners will often tell you that after looking at what they needed to when faced with making a decision, they ended up making the final call on their gut feel.

I am suggesting that I believe the reason we have a

gut feel, is to use it. Just in the same way that we can feel if something is hot or cold. If I place my hand on the stove and feel that it's really hot, I quickly move my hand to avoid getting burned. I act based on a sensation (move or you will have a burned hand buddy).

In the same way, I believe we must use our gut feel.

Consider what others have to say but ultimately I would suggest that like most winners, trust your intuition. Trust your gut and push through with your thoughts.

I have always found my gut feel to be right.

I'm sure you will too.

Take a moment to reflect on this truth. Consciously live this truth in week 15.

Winning Truth Number

16

Make the Promise

I once wrote to myself on a big piece of paper 'I will always win, because I will never quit.' It's not because I am better than anyone, it's not because I am smarter than anyone and it's not because I have more resources than anyone. It's because I will keep standing long after everyone has left the game. I will be standing and working on my vision right to the last breath. That's the commitment I have made to myself. In my mind, I am Rocky Balboa, the last man standing when it comes to fighting for that world title belt — *my dream.*

Everyone around you will want to achieve their goals and dreams, but unfortunately they give up when the going gets tough. When the going gets tough, the tough must fight back. When the going gets tough, you must remember that the game of life is not a game of convenience. If it were, everyone would win. It's a game of mental toughness.

Will Smith once said in an interview that he could beat anyone on a treadmill. It wasn't because he was the fittest person in the world, but purely because he would outlast any challenger by being so committed to never giving up.

Every winner has made a promise, be it in private or in public, and that is to never ever ever ever give up, no matter what. They have locked in on their target, and will not stop until they get to it. They might be delayed, they might be challenged beyond their beliefs, they might be forced to take alternative routes, but whatever happens they are committed to their promise, and will never break it.

Whatever you choose to do in life, make a promise to stick in all the way. Make a commitment to never give yourself the option of giving up. If failure was not an option and success is your only option, then you are forced to succeed. Every winner I have come across in life has had to outlast, outrun and outwit the challenges they faced. They had the tenacity to see themselves through the finish line of any race they chose to start.

Do you know the percentage of people who would have started this book and will never finish it? Believe it or not probably over 75%. I look forward to hearing that you are part of the 25% who have chosen to cross the finish line.

Winners have one exit strategy, and that's not succumbing to challenges and reasons. Their only exit strategy is achieving what they set out to do.

To be a winner in any aspect of your life, you must first make that promise.

Take a moment to reflect on this truth.
Consciously live this truth in week 16.

Winning Truth Number

17

A Battlefield

I once met a friend of mine in a hotel lobby. After exchanging pleasantries and greetings, our talks drifted to the state of Economy. We agreed that although things were tough, opportunities were plenty. They were simply repackaged and presented in different forms.

My friend then made an interesting comment. He said, 'Life is not a hotel. Life is a battlefield. You must fight through life. Most people think life to be the equivalent of a seven star hotel service. It just doesn't work that way.'

His words were very true. Life indeed is a game, and like any game, you have to actively play. In any game, just when you think you know what will happen next, something of a different nature occurs. That's what makes it interesting, not knowing what's around the corner, having to deal with challenges, and do so effectively. You can't expect things to be served to you (at least initially). You have to get out there and play.

Winners know that life is a battlefield, and there will be expected and unexpected twists and turns.

Life is full of challenges. Smile in the face of challenges and adversities. If you are faced with a tough situation, be sure that you are the person that can handle it. For I believe we are all given challenges and hardships based on our abilities to handle them. I don't believe that we are ever faced with a situation that we are unable to handle, even though it may feel like it at the time.

Sometimes you expect to rise to the top with a hot air balloon, but due to some technical difficulties you are left stranded on the ground searching for a solution, only to be flown up to the moon in a space shuttle. All this was possible just because you had a desire and were focussed on getting to the top and not on the challenge like the majority do.

It's through challenges that winners' thoughts are invoked. Through challenges, winners are inspired to think. Through challenges winners turn their dreams into reality. Through challenges, winners begin to lead. Through challenges, winners set forth towards victory, for nothing is sweeter than winning, especially when the odds are stacked against them.

Whatever you're into, strap up your boots and start playing. Expect and welcome challenges into your life. This is the game of life, and it's definitely no seven star hotel. Indeed it's a battlefield.

Take a moment to reflect on this truth.
Consciously live this truth in week 17.

Winning Truth Number

18

Work Your Passion

We all have passions in life. The difference is winners do what they are passionate about when most people don't. Winners work their passion, and hence they never see what they do as a chore. The majority however feels like every task in their life is an unpleasant one. It's no wonder most people are frustrated, tired and void of energy.

Coming back to weight loss, I personally wanted to lose a bit of weight and get fit at the same time. Back then, I despised doing cardio but knew that I had to burn calories. So I thought I would achieve my goal by picking something I would enjoy, something I would love. A friend suggested I join him for a few games of badminton, and before I knew it, I was hooked.

I was so passionate about being a cut above the rest, that at any given opportunity given a chance I would be on. I would usually be called to be a substitute for a social team. On Sunday mornings I was there to play solidly (and usually the first to get to the courts) until I was asked to leave the court and let others play. When anyone needed a spare person to fill in, I would rush to play. I was simply so excited about every opportunity I was given.

When I first started playing I recall noticing many of the players had much more talent, potential and practice time than me. Yet within a short time I had reached their playing level. Obviously many weren't as passionate about it as I was. What they had in skills and talents, I compensated with my passion. Needless to say, I also lost the weight as a side benefit (talk about a win win)

In life, passion outweighs both talent and ability. It's for this reason that you would see many talented people often wondering how someone with a lot less ability or talent got to where they are. They had a reason, a fire.

When you are passionate about something, you are excited. Every task is seen as a breeze. Procrastination is at a minimal. You are not worried about failure; you are too caught up in doing what you are passionate about. Your decisions are not based on the fear of losing rather based on the pleasure of achieving the tasks and getting to the set goals.

Life and whatever you do in your time in this world should not be a chore. You will be spending a lot of time doing it anyway. Every moment should be fuelled by your passion. It's your reason. It's your *why*. When you have passion, you make things happen.

Take a moment to reflect on this truth. Consciously live this truth in week 18.

Winning Truth Number

19

The Oven

I have a friend who is a great baker and whenever we visit her place, she brings out beautiful pieces of chocolate cakes. Amazed by the texture and quality, I once asked her how it was made. She gave me the recipe and then mentioned that the crucial part was actually the time (and temperature) she left them in the oven to get it just right. She emphasized the importance of giving it the time for the ingredients to fall into place.

That struck a chord in me. So many times people put in the ingredients of their desired cake and yet are disappointed because they have not given their efforts time to set. They did not give their ingredients the 45 minutes needed to turn it into this beautiful tasty chocolate cake. They expected their cake to be ready instantly.

How much time would you need to spend to win? How much time should you allow for? How long it would take for you to pursue your passion and make it a reality? How long would your 45 minutes equate to in real life?

All very good questions, but one where there is no

answer. I don't know how long it will take you, but guess what, it doesn't matter. As long as you are making the right moves, doing the right things, learning your way forward, doing the numbers, training hard, working your passion, then you will reach a point when the alarm rings to inform you that your 45 minutes are over, and that your cake is indeed ready.

The cliché that good things take time holds true. It might be a day; it might be a week, a month or even a year. It may take you a lifetime, but you will get there, and most important of all you will be someone who enjoys the process, for if you ask anyone who bakes a tasty cake, they will tell you that it's in the baking process that they get the greatest pleasure.

When everyone wants things *now now now*. Winners learn to take action; whilst knowing that their time will come. Keep doing what you need to do and you will achieve your result.

Just as you would have the patience and understanding that a fertilized egg requires nine months before a baby is born, you must develop the patience to know that your time will come, as long as you're putting in the right ingredients.

It is not a question of if, but a matter of when.

Take a moment to reflect on this truth.
Consciously live this truth in week 19.

Winning Truth Number

20

The Certainty of Uncertainty

As humans we have a number of needs. Two of those needs are 1. the need for certainty and 2. the need for uncertainty. The need for certainty brings about peace of mind, and the need for uncertainty brings about life.

Many strive to have as much certainty in their life as possible. They are afraid of uncertainty. There are two challenges that arise from this.

First of all, life would be plain boring if everything was certain. Secondly, the more certainty you require in life, the more chance there is that you will be let down and unhappy. This is because you will be going against the flow of reality. Much of life is uncertain and those who win are the ones who accept and learn to dance to the rhythm of whatever music the day decides to play.

Life will continuously throw you challenges. Some you will expect, most you won't. Some will come at a time where you feel you can handle them, most will come when you least want them to.

As any winner would, you must be quick to adapt to

best serve the purpose of what you set out to do. More importantly, you must always be on the look out for change, so that you are at the forefront rather than the tail end of it.

If something happens in your world, believe that it has happened for a good reason. Rather than asking, 'Why has this happened to me?' ask a more useful question such as, *'How can I benefit from this?'*

Winners believe everything that happens in their life isn't just a mere accident. They are incidents, some of which are out of control, while others are as a result of their thoughts and actions.

When the majority of people get bogged down about negative events in their lives, winners see past it into the distance taking on lessons learned. Every event is a lesson to help them move stronger and smarter.

Those who embrace and turn uncertainty in their favor will come out as winners in a world filled with those trying (and failing) to control things that are out of their reach.

You can only control you.

Uncertainty is part of the game. The sooner you accept this, the sooner you can be at peace with yourself.

Let go. Have fun with uncertainty because when you learn to do so, you will be certain to win.

Take a moment to reflect on this truth. Consciously live this truth in week 20.

Winning Truth Number

21

More than a Game of One

One day on a thirty minute break whilst working at McDonalds, I remember looking up after having devoured my lunch. The pin- up note read:

TEAM = Together Everyone Achieves More

It made enough sense to me in the context of working at McDonalds, after all we all worked together to ensure the restaurant functioned smoothly.

However years down the road, I realized that winners win through the power of having the right team. Winners understand the importance and difference having a winning team can make. It's more than just having a bunch of people around them.

Often people look at winners as the be all and end all. They fail to see the people behind the scenes that have undeniably helped in elevating the winner. These are the people in the foreground and many that are in the background. These are the people that make it happen. These are the people that are often not made public to the eye or even made a mention of. However, they constitute the pillars with which any winning individual can stand on and perform at their very best, knowing that they will be supported through thick and thin.

Whatever you're into, the people around you make all the difference. If you are an athlete, then the right coach, trainer, nutritionist is crucial. If you are a CEO, then the right mix of lawyers, accountants and advisors are imperative. Donald Trump has a winning team. 50 Cent has a winning team. Oprah Winfrey has a winning team. Steven Spielberg has a winning team. Tiger Woods has a winning team.

The power you can attain from having the right people around you is beyond the comprehension of most people. Your team can be in the form of a support group, mastermind, or a circle of winning minds. Whether you are starting off or well on your way to winning, it's paramount to have the right circle (one of the reasons we have created the exclusive Winners Inner Circle which you can check out on www.KevinAbdulrahman.com).

Winners understand that the game is not played solo. They need a team and the members need to be great. They need to be on par with the winner, and in fact in most cases, need to be better than the winner (in their field of expertise). That's why you have them there in the first place. A team complements the winners' strength and provides the support needed for continuous growth.

A well-orchestrated team can play the masterpiece you desire.

Take a moment to reflect on this truth.
Consciously live this truth in week 21.

Winning Truth Number

22

Failure is the Foundation

At some point in our lives, we are all gripped with a crippling fear. This crippling fear is that of failure. This fear is so appalling that it stops the majority of people from even taking the initial step. It boggles me, so many out there will never take a step towards their dreams because they are too afraid of failing.

Yes the idea of failing is a scary and daunting thought. After all who wants to fail? Certainly no one wants to be associated with failure and unfortunately it's for that reason that many never capitalise on their talent and potential. Their worry often cripples them.

Winners know that standing still is a bigger failure when compared to failing whilst moving forward. Because if you give something a go and fail, you have at least walked away with valuable lessons, and therefore are ahead.

We tend to look at the world's greatest individuals and admire them for their success. What many don't realize are the numerous failures they have had to experience along the way. Take for example Michael

Jordan, a basketball great and a certain winner in all our minds. To this day many are in awe of him and his achievements on the court. He's not only the inspiration of many current basketball champions, but just about every young aspiring kid out there interested in the sport.

This is what Michael had to say about the reason for his success, *'I have missed more than nine thousand shots in my career. I have lost almost three hundred games. On twenty-six occasions, I have been entrusted to take the game's winning shot, and I missed. I have failed over and over again in my life. And that is precisely why I succeed.'*

Every winner will tell you of all the times they have failed. They will tell you about the failures they had to endure for the success they have today. They will share with you that the rewards of getting what they want far outweighs the failures they have had to face. They will declare that their failures have been the foundation for their success.

Winners expect and embrace failures as something that will remain constant throughout their lives. No matter how successful they are in whatever they do, they will have the failures to go alongside it.

Every winner out there has had to first become a Master of Failure before enjoying the winning side of life.

**Take a moment to reflect on this truth.
Consciously live this truth in week 22.**

Winning Truth Number

23

The Purpose

In my first book *Winning The Game Of Life* I mentioned that most people spend more time doing their hair or planning their summer holidays than actually planning their lives. As part of that the requisite of important planning is to first ask and understand, 'what is your purpose'?

Why is it important for you to know your purpose? The state that you can see most people are in should be enough of an answer. Unhappy, unfulfilled, hating what they do, will drop everything at the chance of escapism (sadly through substance abuse and even lingering purposelessly online) are but a few examples of how many are unfortunately living their life.

All Winners have a sense of purpose. They have thought of the things they can have, do and give in this world. They have narrowed it down to and clarified their answers to the questions, 'What do I want? And why do I want to do it'? Having that clarity gives them the force to begin, hang in and achieve their goals.

Having purpose is having clarity of where you want

to head and knowing without a shadow of doubt that it's what you want to throw yourself in whole heartedly.

Is this an overnight process? I wish I could give you an answer. Some of you will know your purpose already, whilst others will take hours, days and if not weeks. But whatever the time you need, invest it in discovering yourself and finding out what will make you tick. Only when you find your reason, your purpose, something greater than yourself, can you begin your journey of winning.

So here are some questions to get you started. Grab some paper (or a blank book) and start writing. Write the answers to the questions below. Write anything that comes to your mind. Write freely, and with no judgment. Just write. In your writing will be your answer.

What is your aim in life? What one thing would you like to achieve in your life? What will ultimately make you happy? How can you contribute in the long term to something that is far bigger than you? Why do you want to do what you want to do? What joy will you get out of it? What will you be missing out on as a result of pursuing what you want? Is it worth it? Is it something you love, and are good at (or can be good at with practice)?

This Truth is a truth that will require you to spend time searching from within.

Take a moment to reflect on this truth. Consciously live this truth in week 23.

Winning Truth Number

24

The Signal and Picture

Our lives are filled with events (big and small) that occur on a daily basis. That's the beauty of life. With so much going on, it requires those with a Winning Mind to stay on course without being distracted by surrounding influences. If you are not focussed you will tend to lag behind in your commitments, your tasks and also achieving your goals. To be productive in your personal and professional life, you need to be focussed and able to deflect life's distractions.

Think of the signal that streams to your satellite dish. When uninterrupted, it gives you a crystal clear picture on your TV. What happens when there is interference in the signal, due to say wind or thunderstorms? The signal is interrupted and as a result, the picture on the screen is affected.

The wind and thunderstorms are the plenty of distractions you get in life. The signal is your focus. The picture on the screen is your result.

Sometimes it seems like you are getting ahead by having so much on your plate, but focussing on completing one task at a time actually helps you achieve more. It may be boring, it may look dull, but you will achieve more, one task at a time. I see so many young entrepreneurs who are always looking for the next best thing, who are always trying to put deals together, who feel that they need to have their fingers in every single pie that they hear of. What they don't realize is their energy is dissipated and they can't achieve the higher result they would have if focussed on a single task at a time.

A well known icon focussed his skill of picking and buying stocks in undervalued companies and watched them flourish in their due time. As a result he amassed a great deal of wealth. That man is Warren Buffet, the second richest man in the world. He applied the simple principle of focus.

Winners know that they become what they focus on most of the time. If you are unhappy with the picture on your TV screen, you change channels or reposition your satellite to pick up the right signal.

Winners know that every day spent focussing on their end reward moves them one step closer to attaining their goals. No matter how minute the results, by focussing more, you will see yourself achieving more.

Choose the picture you desire to have and ensure you have an uninterrupted signal.

**Take a moment to reflect on this truth.
Consciously live this truth in week 24.**

Winning Truth Number

25

Draw a Line in the Sand

As a kid I had a choice of two beach balls to play with. There was a dull brown ball that I had and a bright ball that I got from a family friend.

As a three year old, I spent the first day distraught at this dilemma. I would play with the colourful ball, and then feel guilty about not playing with the brown ball. So I would go back to spend some time with the brown ball before turning to the bright ball again.

This went on for the whole day, and by the end of it all, I remember feeling exhausted about having to juggle two beach balls.

I did what winners do. I made up my mind once and for all. It was tough, but a decision had to be made. At three years of age, I knew I couldn't move forward with being indecisive about which ball to befriend and play with.

Winners make up their mind.

Yes, the majority of people make their minds up regularly, but unfortunately they play a game of beach volley. One day they are on one side of the net, and the next day they are on the other side. Winners makes serious decisions. They make the tough decisions and they stick with it.

For example, a winner will choose to excel in a sport or compete at an Olympics. Through their tenure, when it comes to being on a strict diet, working out, traveling the globe to compete, the question as to 'whether they should do it or not' never pops up. They have already made up their mind, and everything they do is to serve that purpose.

Similarly when winners choose to build a successful organization, they have made up their minds to do so. When it comes to the numerous choices they will be required to make, it will be relatively easy for them, as they will opt in for the choices that are in line with what they decided they would do.

Draw a line in the sand and decide where you want to stand.

I made a decision at three. It's time you made some serious decisions like any winner would.

Winning starts with a decision. Make one, and then back it up with massive action.

Take a moment to reflect on this truth. Consciously live this truth in week 25.

Winning Truth Number

26

Lucky Indeed

Some people just seem to have all the luck. You are lucky to be a successful business person. You are lucky to have a great family. You are lucky that you are doing what you love in life. You are lucky that you haven't been hurt by the crisis. You are lucky because you are a born orator. You are lucky to have won the contest. You are lucky to have sealed some of the biggest deals around.

Most people will only conveniently see the end result? They don't see the choices winners had to make, the time and money they invested, the blood, sweat and tears put in, the determination to keep pushing and much much more to be where they are today.

I was once asked in an interview whether our results stemmed from luck or hard work?

Luck of course, I replied. You should've seen the room. For a few seconds the room was so silent that I could hear the conversation occurring up the road. I then said, 'seriously speaking it's both'.

After all what does luck mean? You would have

heard many say that luck is found at the crossroads of preparation and opportunity.

A wise person once shared with me a definition of Luck that has since stuck with me. He said L.U.C.K stands for Laboring Under Correct Knowledge. Winners work hard doing the right things and that's why they are lucky.

My question to you is, are you Labouring Under Correct Knowledge?

I believe that the harder you work, the luckier you get, as long as you are taking the right steps. You have to ask yourself, 'based on what I want, am I doing the right things that will get me to be lucky'?

You see, it's like saying, you want to put on weight and you are not taking in enough calories, or a problem people are more familiar with – you want to lose weight and still are on take-away and donut diets. You have to do the right things in line with what you want in your life.

I would like to suggest that in most instances it is your choices that determine your luck.

Take a moment to reflect on this truth.
Consciously live this truth in week 26.

Winning Truth Number

27

Positivity Will Only Take You So Far

The other day I was invited over for a cup of coffee at a friend's place, as we had not met for a long time. Naturally, when we met she was quite excited. We sat and started chatting about old times. Whilst talking she went to make a pot of coffee, she picked up the kettle, filled it up with water and placed it on its base on the kitchen bench top.

Fifteen minutes later I politely pointed out that though she had turned the kettle on, there was no sign of the water boiling.

I thought it would be best for me to get up and check on things. Sure enough the kettle seemed to be in working condition, it was switched on and there certainly was water in it. However, I soon realized that my friend had forgotten to plug in the kettle.

There I was, all along, waiting for a steaming cup of hot coffee only to find out that the kettle chord was unplugged.

The point I'm coming to is that the people who know

me personally and professionally know me as Mr. Positive.

I am a guy who will always see an upside in a situation, but I can tell you something that I also am very aware of. No matter how positive I was, that kettle was not going to boil anytime soon (actually never) unless it was plugged in.

It made me think about life and how many people want their kettle to boil and yet have it unplugged. They seem to think just because they want it to boil, or since they have done a certain action everything else will fall into place or happen on its own.

As much as I believe in being positive (I'm a big advocate), I'm the first to say that it will only get you so far. Sure you need to be positive in life, and expect the best, but you must back it up with action.

Turning on the kettle is part of the equation but you need to make sure it's plugged in.

I believe that by now you must have realized that this book is action orientated, from the preface and right through every truth.

Unlike the kettle, the goals you set out to accomplish will have many more elements that require action, so you must always ensure that you are taking the right action at the right time.

Take a moment to reflect on this truth.
Consciously live this truth in week 27.

Winning Truth Number

28

The Consistent Tortoise

Most people want a lot of things. They want to win in their lives both personally and professionally, and yet won't do what they need to do as discussed in the first chapter.

Take for example some people who work from home or run an Internet business. They are motivated (which is why they started one). They will make calls, work through the early hours of the morning, meet with people, do orders, and tackle the challenges they come across. Compared to many in the industry they might start off at ten times the pace. However after a short while, they are disappointed, become complacent, or forget the reason they got motivated in the first place and sadly many stop three meters short of their gold pot.

Other people tend to get motivated then go on an action spurt. But just like opening a bottle of fizzy drink, they fizz out at the first rejection they face. They are flat by the next morning. Now it may sound like I'm being over dramatic but it's a fact. Some would last a few days and then once they are off their high, they stop doing what they set out to do.

In any case, we witness inconsistencies, and winning requires the commitment of being consistent. Whether you are fast or slow, that is irrelevant. It's not about motivated spikes, it's about longevity. What is relevant and of importance is the truth that consistency is a must if you are serious about winning. The game of life is not about the spurts of effort and energy you put in, but consistent persistence in pursuing the goal.

Just ask any winner and they will tell you that their consistent effort is a key reason for their win. They do something everyday towards their goal.

You might find it challenging to write a book or start a business, but if you do just a little bit everyday, at the end of a year or two, you have done a whole lot. And that whole lot equates to tangible results that you will be able to see.

Take one consistent step after another, and you will build a massive result.

Remember the tortoise always wins because it's consistent in moving towards its destination. No matter how slow you may feel it to be, if you keep on doing the right things, sooner or later, you will enjoy your win.

Winning is more than just a one hit wonder. It's in the consistent actions.

Take a moment to reflect on this truth.
Consciously live this truth in week 28.

Winning Truth Number

29

The Value in Understanding Values

Whether we are conscious of it or not, we all have values that govern our actions. What you value is not necessarily what someone else values and vice versa. These values dictate our preferences, desires and goals that are important for us.

On the surface, some people would rather eat a range of tasty food over buying and wearing new clothes all the time (that's definitely me). Others prefer buying gizmos instead of traveling the world and experiencing different cultures. For example I enjoy buying lattes that help me relax and write, rather than buying a new pair of shoes every week. I know a particular friend who is the complete opposite.

Going beneath these surface actions, they are all dictated by decisions, which are dictated by our values. You will most certainly know people who are completely unhappy with their life, or at least an element of their life. The chances are it's because they are not functioning in line with their set of values.

Everyone has a set of values (they simply might not be aware of their list and its order) and more importantly, we all have different priorities for those values. Think of it on a scale of 1 to 10.

For instance your values would be 1. Family 2. Time freedom 3. Doing what you love 4. Money.

For the next person it could be 1. Money 2. Time freedom 3. Doing what they love and 4. Family.

Some of you are thinking, 'Hang on a second Kevin, aren't they all the same?'

Indeed, we may share similar values, but it is the weight we give each one that matters. It's the priority we give to these values which distinguishes us and the actions we take. This is something you must understand if you like to drive yourself to maximum potential.

Winners understand their order of values and work in alignment with them. You must know the weight of your values and ensure that you are working in line with them. Write up your values from 1 to 10 (1 being most important), and then ensure that all the actions you take are in line with your values. Work in line with your values and you will begin to witness massive results, all whilst being happy and in peace with yourself.

Take a moment to reflect on this truth. Consciously live this truth in week 29.

Winning Truth Number

30

Work Less, Get More

Doesn't that sound like something of a dream? Work less and yet get more.

That's exactly what winners do.

They do so by first of all finding out what they are:

1. Good at 2. Love to do.

Some people usually end up doing what they are good at but have no true love for it. Others do what they love, but sadly they are just not good at it. For example I vividly remember a very successful business lady who was doing what she did because she was good at it and it paid well, however she hated it (and hate is a strong word). Another example is that I would have loved to sing professionally but sadly I haven't been gifted in that field and so no matter how much I love it, it won't be something I would be good at.

Winners spend their time searching until they find (and there is something for every one of us) what they are good at and love to do.

By doing what you are good at and love to do, you

end up gaining much more and working much less. Some would even work more (wait a minute it sounds like I'm contradicting myself), but because you will love what you do, it won't feel that you are working more.

After all, it actually is never about how many hours you are putting in; it's really how you *feel* about it.

You would have had an experience in your life where you did a task or project, and working at it seemed like a breeze. Sure you might have faced challenges, but because it was something you loved doing, those challenges were only considered as mere road bumps. Hours went by and it felt like minutes. Weeks may have gone by and it only felt like a weekend. The point is you really enjoyed it. In these instances you are the most creative and there is nothing stopping you.

What matters for any winner is the *feel* and it is in these moments that they have some of their best performances resulting in amazing wins.

Love it, and work it.

In there lies your ultimate win.

Take a moment to reflect on this truth.
Consciously live this truth in week 30.

Winning Truth Number 31

Choose the Right Station

If life was a metro station, and most people got off at the ATNA station.

How many times have you heard people tell you about all the things they want to do, and end up doing nothing? Well guess what, they certainly don't constitute winners. They are definitely those who get off at the ATNA station.

Good intentions mean nothing. Intentions don't bring you results and the world has no shortage of people who only have good intentions. Some realize that sooner or later, that the ATNA station serves no purpose, and to be able to enjoy life for what it is, they will benefit from choosing an alternative station.

Winners get off at a different station. Their station is LTMA. And in case you are wondering what the acronym of the stations are:

ATNA = 'All Talk No Action'

LTMA = 'Less Talk More Action'

Most people relish in the caliber of their conversations. They are crippled with the disease of thinking things repeatedly over and over again. You think you get the drift?

Winners act more than they think. They move with what they know. They don't make time for idle chat. You will notice them to be the quiet ones whose greatest joy is in getting down to business and attaining a winning result.

Winners take control, by making decisions and more importantly taking action. Compare that with the 'watch from the sidelines and hope' approach of the majority. Indeed winners do hope for the best, but their hope has a higher chance of becoming a reality because of the actions they take.

Wait and see is not a winning action.

I trust by now, you are living each truth that you have read so far in this book.

The true value of each truth will come out based on the actions you take.

Take a moment to reflect on this truth.
Consciously live this truth in week 31.

Winning Truth Number

32

Really Don't Care

What do you think Kevin?

I am always asked by a lot of clients about my thoughts regarding projects that they are considering. On one occasion I had a reader of one of my books e-mail me with a message that read,

'I am leading the global expansion of a company who saves the average person $5-15 at the pump, truckers $100, reduces emissions by 30-100%, and extends the life of any engine by years, gas or diesel. This is non toxic, Very 'green', and costs people much more not to use... Do you think there is money to be made on a product that does this? I enjoy networking and teaching people how to retire in 1-3 years. You seem very inspirational, and I look forward to your response.'

This is one of the plenty of e-mails my team fields on a weekly basis. I chose to reply to this personally. I said,

> *Dear friend,*
> *You are the one who has chosen to embark on this project. Do You think there is money to be*

made on the product? Don't ask me for my opinion, because it will be based on my knowledge, limitations, beliefs, skills and abilities. What I believe is that if one has done their due diligence on a project, have the vision of attaining their end reward and have a burning desire to achieve it then they are destined to succeed. Because no matter what I think, and no matter who thinks what, the only person whose thoughts matter is the person who will embark on their chosen journey. Even the best of people who thought a project won't work, were proven wrong by those who knew they could make it work. I hope you realize the message within this message.

In friendship

Kevin Abdulrahman

Too many times people ask others for their opinions and thoughts when it's pointless to do so (this is different from constructive feedback).

Suppose I replied saying, that I didn't think it was viable. Should you give up on something if you have a clear vision of turning it into a success? What if I said, 'yeah I think its great' but you lack the vision, guts and determination to see it through? In any case, thoughts and opinions shouldn't matter. If you have a crystal clear vision and you will back it up with action and determination of never ever giving up, then success is yours for the taking.

Winners do not care about what other people think

of them or their chosen passion. As long as they are happy within themselves, and know that in their heart they are doing the right thing, then they push forward with it.

Take a moment to reflect on this truth. Consciously live this truth in week 32.

Winning Truth Number

33

It's Never Personal

I must have approached over 100 publishers for my first book *Winning The Game Of Life.* To say that I had enjoyed an array of rejections is an understatement. There were folks who never replied back, some who kindly rejected it and then there were those who weren't so kind about it. But oh! I kept on pushing past all the rejections until my book got to the hands of a well known publicist in the States who said 'Hang on a second, you've got something here', and within days we had a publishing deal on the table.

As I travel the world training individuals and organizations, I come across some immensely talented people in different fields. Their talent is however buried under a pile of rejections they have faced. Sadly they have taken it personally. In every challenging situation where rejections are offered left right and center, the first exit door that appears to many is the one that reads, 'Give up now. Save yourself further headaches and heartburns'. The difference between those succeeding and the ones who give up is one thing, their ability to deal with rejections. The majority of people take rejection personally. Winners know that rejection is part of the process.

Only because a few people don't share your views about something, doesn't mean that your idea has no value. All it takes is for one person to see it, and that person is You. There are countless examples of people who started off being the only ones who visualized the power of their skills, abilities, products or services they had. It took them several rejections before they had a breakthrough. Here is the key though, they persevered passed all the rejections and kept pushing forward without taking it to heart.

If we were all to take rejection to heart then we wouldn't have the pleasure of having a computer on every desk, we would still be riding horses instead of cars, the Harry Potter franchise wouldn't be around, Denzel Washington wouldn't be one of the highest paid actors of his time, and certainly we wouldn't have many of the things we take for granted that were initially laughed at and blatantly rejected in its infancy.

Always remember that what is being rejected is your idea or your offering, not you. Rejection stems from other peoples limitations, beliefs, fears and different perspective on things. Think of a time when you were on a plane and the steward or stewardess did their rounds offering tea or coffee. You would have declined their offer at some stage and it would be fair to say that they face numerous rejections. However I don't believe that they take it personally. They understand that their offer of tea and coffee is what is being rejected, nothing more. You too should learn to never take rejections to heart.

Take a moment to reflect on this truth. Consciously live this truth in week 33.

Winning Truth Number

34

Get to the Edge and the PUSH

A friend once told me about a quote he had read somewhere. It said, 'If you are not living on the edge, you're taking up too much space.'

As you are well aware, we are all creatures of routine. Most people are operating their day to day lives as though on autopilot, without getting to the edge and really pushing their boundaries to test their true abilities. Sadly this comfort zone is where many remain trapped in for their entire lives only to look back (if they ever get the opportunity) and realize that what was deemed as a comfort zone was in fact *robbed of a full* life zone. To them, life was painful, but not painful enough. Things were good but not great. They fell into what they happened to be good at, rather than do something they were passionate about. Complacency and fear kept these people within the framework of living a life of comfortable misery.

If there is one guarantee that I can give you right now, it will be this. I can guarantee that every winner has had to get to the edge and push through his or her boundaries. They have had to test their potential and fail repeatedly one way or another. Winners would rather set a stretched goal and achieve 80% of it, thereby constituting failure in the eyes of many, rather than setting a goal that is easily achievable from the outset (how unexciting). Testing one's true ability and only getting 80% of the way is a win in my eyes.

There is no joy in setting a goal that in your mind you can achieve easily. Deep down in your heart you know that it would've never got out the best in you. The best of you will always be brought out by being stretched. It doesn't have to be so far out of reach, but it certainly needs to bring out what you would deem uncomfortable, testing your knowledge, abilities and skills.

Winners push to break through. They push to get out of their comfort zone. They become uncomfortable and as soon as it becomes their standard benchmark, they push to break through again. Winners are always on a journey of discovering how much more they are able to do. The Beijing Olympics was a brilliant example showcasing winners like Michael Phelps who attained a record 8 gold medals and Usain the lightening Bolt who broke three world records. Not only did they break records, but they continuously strive to get to their edge, and push.

You must learn to get comfortable becoming uncomfortable. By constantly stretching beyond your day-to-day comfort levels, you will amaze yourself as to how much more exists within you. There is much more in you waiting to be unlocked. Go ahead and unleash yourself to the world.

Take a moment to reflect on this truth. Consciously live this truth in week 34.

Winning Truth Number

35

Do Something You Know You Can Do

Think of a time when you were really excited about doing a task. You would have not liked it but more importantly in your mind, it was achievable.

Knowing that you can achieve is imperative. The times you've given up on a goal is when you subconsciously thought that 'it was impossible' or you wouldn't be able to achieve it. To avoid disappointment and feeling like a failure, you avoided it all together by doing what? Nothing!!! This in turn didn't serve your purpose of winning, did it?

Let me give you a personal example. At one point I was on the heavy side and I wanted to lose weight. However every time I looked in the mirror I would see this fat slob (Hey, that was the comment that was going in my head). I wanted to look and feel good but yet couldn't see myself losing all that weight. So for two years I did nothing.

One day, I thought to myself, what if I didn't think of

the end result? What if I went to the gym and watched a 30 minute TV show whilst on a treadmill everyday. That was something I could do. After all, I would be so engrossed on what was on TV, that I wouldn't realize a 30 minute workout. It was a small goal but it was a step in the right direction and in my mind, it was achievable. I realized that this way, I am bound to be ahead at the end of two years. Sure it is not as good as looking great in 12 weeks like many weight challenges out there. But in reality, two years had already slipped. I was overweight and unhappy. Thirty minutes was something I could do, and that's how I started. Eventually, after 12 months, I had reached my larger goal and lost the 19 kilograms I wanted to. I got to my unachievable goal by doing small achievable tasks, i.e I knew I could do it.

What have you been putting off ? You may have gotten excited about it, but stopped because you got anxiety attacks or a feeling of being completely overwhelmed at the thought of starting because the thought of failing occurred?

The best way to create breakthrough results is to break down what you want to small achievable tasks and focus solely on them. That way, you can bring back the bounce in your step when doing each smaller task. By achieving these smaller tasks, you will feel good, become confident, and will be aching to take on the next challenge. One step at a time, you can conquer mini tasks and challenges, ultimately reaching a major goal.

Break down your big goals to smaller ones, and then

do it without thinking any further than the task at hand. Put that bounce in your step and get on with it. Doing so continuously, will get you to your larger goals over time.

Take a moment to reflect on this truth. Consciously live this truth in week 35.

Winning Truth Number

36

Only One Contestant

It's in our nature to compare ourselves to people around us. We compare and get compared with all the time. We are compared to siblings, friends, parents, cousins, role models, the stranger down the road and even the neighbour's cat. Consciously or subconsciously we are mistakenly compared in our societies. This is the way most of us were brought up and have been subjected to.

Most people usually compare themselves with others and feel that there is something wrong with them. There is nothing wrong with you. We are all different. I say this, because you must always remember that you have been blessed with a set of skills and abilities. You have been subjected to different situations and as a result have developed and excelled in different areas (if you haven't, then you sure can).

Life is a game. Each and every one of us is playing a different game. Most times we excel in different things. Success is winning, and your definition of winning will be different to the next person. Some of us are faster in certain aspects, and slower in others. No two people are the same, so why compare?

Comparing is like cancer. Stay away from it.

Winners use others success stories as inspiration to drive them, not as comparison. Winners know that winning is about being the best that one can be. Don't be hard on yourself for your results. You can only move forward and learn from it. Use other people's success stories as inspiration and if you are serious then change your beliefs, change your thoughts, change your decisions and change your actions to suit your purpose.

You call the shots as to where the start and finish lines are drawn. There is only one contestant in this race. In fact it's not even a race, it's a journey. A journey where you have the opportunity to be the best you can be, do the best that you can do, and give back the best that you can give back in your time on this planet.

Your biggest challenge is to be able to control your mind, to control your emotions, to be able to act when you least want to do and to let go when you don't.

The biggest game you will ever play is the game in your mind.

Master your mind, and you will master your world.

Take a moment to reflect on this truth.
Consciously live this truth in week 36.

Winning Truth Number

37

You Are Worth It

I come across thousands and thousands of people who are constantly unhappy about what they get out of their employment and their businesses, relationships and friendship.

In all cases, I hear a common statement being made. The majority of people say 'I'm worth more' but with a doubt in their mind. They all scream, 'I'm worth more'. But what lingers in their mind is, 'I'm not good enough, or I don't deserve better'.

Many seek reassurance of their worth from friends, colleagues, bosses at work or partners in life. You receive what you deserve. How you treat yourself is usually reflected in how others treat you. If you respect yourself, you will undoubtedly get respect. If you love yourself, you will certainly be loved. If you are getting paid a certain amount from your employment or business then it's a direct result of what you are doing. You deserve what you are worth right now.

Winners know their worth without a shadow of doubt. In knowing so, they project it, and therefore command it both directly, and more so indirectly. If you really feel that you deserve more, then your thoughts and actions must say it too. You must without a doubt, believe (remember that earlier truth) that you deserve more and therefore do what you need to do to achieve that.

The value others give you is the value you give yourself. The choices you make, the actions you take, the attitude you have towards yourself, the inner talk you have with yourself, is all affected by the self worth you have of yourself. If you have a high self worth, then you will have a positive attitude, you will think positive empowering thoughts and will act accordingly. If you have a low self worth, then you will have a negative attitude towards yourself.

What is your attitude towards yourself? What sort of inner talk are you having with yourself? Are you talking up or are you talking down to yourself? You must be aware and control your inner talk.

Winners put their own price tags on themselves rather than have anyone help put it on for them. Winners constantly remind themselves about who really indicates their worth. They know it's an inside job.

Who indicates your worth? You do. Always have, always will.

Take a moment to reflect on this truth.
Consciously live this truth in week 37.

Winning Truth Number 38

To Have is to Do. More Importantly It's to Be.

You may admire what someone has done, become or has and set out to do the same. You are inspired and roaring to move ahead in life. You might be inspired by the wealth your friends have acquired, the sporting achievement of Lewis Hamilton, the success of P Diddy, the time freedom that many young couples have through smart home based businesses and the like.

Most people try to model their life after the people around them, whom they consider to be successful and prosperous. They want to *have* what the successful person has, so that they can *do* what they do, in order to *become* just like them. And that's exactly why most people remain in their circle of frustration for years, because they go about the process in the wrong way.

They've got it all mixed up.

Here is the winning truth. You must first *be* the person you are wishing to model (in the way they think and more importantly act), *do* what that person does (and has done to get there) in order to *have* what the person has (the goal).

I recall speaking with a client of mine recently, where he shared with me one of his dreams. He said that he wanted to be the CEO of his own company with interest in 14 sectors of the market. He was very clear about this goal. So we discussed how most people would carry on doing what they are doing hoping to achieve that result. They think that once they are a CEO and have businesses in 14 sectors, only then will they do what's needed and become (behave and act like) the CEO in charge.

I suggested that, in reality, if he were serious about winning, he would have to begin operating his days as if he was already the CEO of a large organization. He didn't have to go out there and buy a new suit, get a new car and get new office premises. All he had to do was to first *become* the CEO in his mind. By then *doing* what a CEO would do, he would end up *having* his dreams.

I shared with him that winners see themselves winning in their mind and then go on to achieve it in the body. The mind is a funny thing, in the sense that when you practice being who you want to be, you end up becoming exactly that, because it can't tell the difference between fact and fiction.

Become the person you inspire to be, do what they would do, and then you will have what they have.

It's really that simple as long as you go about doing it the right way.

**Take a moment to reflect on this truth.
Consciously live this truth in week 38.**

Winning Truth Number

39

The Importance of Breakfast

Many of us dislike being criticized.

Who in their right mind would like to be provoked, be told that their thoughts are wrong or what they are doing isn't up to the mark?

Well, winners do.

It's been said that feedback is the breakfast of champions, yet the majority of people find it difficult to receive true and honest feedbacks as it's a blow to their ego. Winners have developed the ability to accept constructive feedback.

Why? Because for them winning is more important than their ego. They know that it's nothing personal and it's part of winning. I'm referring to constructive feedbacks and only from those who have the experience you lack, have a perspective to share, and more importantly, have your best interest in terms of your goals in mind (This is different from having people tell you what you should and shouldn't be doing in life. Those are mere opinions, and from *Winning The Game Of Life,* you know what to do with opinions).

When was the last time you received constructive feedback for your actions?

If you want to achieve your goals you must be open to hearing how you can possibly improve. You might have a blind spot and the ability to handle constructive feedback could certainly help you. Feedback is a correcting mechanism, to help ensure you are on the right path should you deviate off course, or to further enhance what you are already doing.

Airplanes are usually 'off course' 90% of the time; yet, we make it from one airport to another when we are traveling because of the navigational mechanism that brings it 'on course'. That's exactly the feedback you need.

One of the roles I have as a coach to my clients is to constantly give them constructive feedback based on our conversations with one another. I teach my students to have fun with feedback, as they will learn a lot from it.

Feedback is critical to winning. Avoid being defensive. Embrace the process and learn to listen actively when receiving it. The more you do so, the more honest your feedback will be.

Evaluate your feedbacks and use them to create winning results.

Take a moment to reflect on this truth.
Consciously live this truth in week 39.

Winning Truth Number

40

Choose Your Meanings

We are all used to sending and receiving text messages. How many times have you sent a text message to someone, and because you didn't receive a reply immediately began to think, 'they don't care about me. They are ignoring me. They don't respect me'? Come on, I know you have, because we all have. Subconsciously we associate one of these negative meanings to an event for not receiving a reply straight away.

I will admit that I used to feel a combination of these emotions and would begin to string made up reasons from here to Africa. I would send a text message to my girl expecting a reply within minutes. If I didn't receive a text message I would start getting worked up. I would attach meanings such as 'she doesn't care about me. She would rather be engrossed with her friends than reply to me, etc. etc.' I would feel overwhelmed, get angry, and it was not healthy for our relationship. Then I came to realize, that in many instances she would have either been busy, was with friends, or was plainly out of credit to reply back. I had chosen to give meaning to an event. I did not need to do that. I could have simply thought of a positive reason or no reason at all, and let it slide. Yet, I chose to attach negative meanings and end up feeling like a jack a#$.

We tend to attach a meaning to any event that occurs in life. In most instances, the meanings we attach to an event are based on our upbringing (which means it will usually be different from one person to another) and often we do it subconsciously. I see people give meaning to events and end up carrying the weight of negatively interpreting every event, every hour of every day. It gets so tiring for them, to a point where they snap and are then left wondering why they feel exhausted. Winners know that this is not conducive to winning.

You will never tend to get the full picture of any situation and you are constantly required to make the best decisions moving forward with the information you get and see. Knowing this then, it is always better to look at the brighter side of any event until you gather all the information there is.

You choose the meaning you attach to an event. If something upsets you, makes you angry, overwhelmed or filled with anxiety, ask yourself, 'what meaning am I choosing to give that event'? More importantly 'why am I choosing to give that meaning'? What other meanings could you attach to it? Could you attach a positive meaning or a meaning that will be neutral? You always can.

Winners understand that if they at some point

learned to stick a negative meaning to an event, they can ensure it gets unstuck and replaced with a positive one.

Take a moment to reflect on this truth. Consciously live this truth in week 40.

Winning Truth Number

41

One Blink is All It Takes

How long does it take to change? Ask a winner, and they will tell you that if it serves their purpose then they will change in a heartbeat.

The majority would like to give you a long-winded answer and justification as to why it takes a long time to change. Some will try to say that change is difficult and that it would take a long time. Others will tell you that they can't, and that's just the way that they are. What a load of bull c*@^.

I will suggest that those who are averse to change or crib about it saying that change is a difficult process don't have a strong enough reason to do so. Change can take place in an instance. As soon as you have a strong reason and make a decision, you can change. How quick? A blink, a snap of a finger, a heartbeat quick.

Winners are able to attach an important reason to what they need to do, and their change can be miraculously quick. When push comes to shove, winners change for the better in an instant.

I remember the time when a friend of mine smoked. He started chain smoking in his late teens. Every time we would go to a café, we'd have to sit outside in order for him to smoke. He would talk about quitting but found it too hard to do so. I always told him that he didn't have a strong enough reason to quit. Years went by and between my travels we connected on one occasion. We went to a café to grab a latte and chat like old times. To my surprise he picked a cosy corner inside the café. After a couple of hours of chatting I couldn't contain myself and had to ask. 'How are you coping with not having lit a cigarette'?

He replied, 'Dude, the lady of my life that I've been telling you about, well she is a non-smoker and within a few months of our dating, she told me how much she disliked my breath. I knew that I had to make a choice and let go of one. The lady of my life is worth far more to me than the joy of smoking. I haven't touched a cigarette since nor do I feel the desire to smoke'.

My friend needed a strong reason and he happened to find it in his lady.

How long does it take to really change? Well if you have a strong reason, then the answer is, *now*.

Winners find a strong reason to back their decision to change, and then do so, in a blink.

Take a moment to reflect on this truth.
Consciously live this truth in week 41.

Winning Truth Number

42

Enjoy the Moment

You may have started this book frustrated with life and wanting to win. If only you could have all that you wanted, then you would be at ease, happy and fulfilled. The truths you have read and applied so far are part of becoming that person. However I'm sorry to be the bearer of bad news (I don't make it, I'm merely delivering it to help you become aware), but unless you learn to smell and enjoy the roses today, with all your problems and headaches, then you will never be at ease, happy and fulfilled.

This is a truth that you must learn to work on yourself now.

Nostalgia doesn't serve you. Many are either living everyday in the glory of their past accomplishments or using the hope for a better future as a way of escapism. People use it to get away into a perceived state of elation. And what are they escaping? They are escaping the much-dreaded present.

They go through day-to-day life as zombies, senseless and numb to the world they live in, and the people they interact with. Absent-minded and not being productive are only some of the signs that constitute this issue — tip of the iceberg so to speak.

If you can't enjoy now, the chances are you never enjoyed those (past) moments for what they were either. Now you are nostalgic about it, but are repeating the same mistake as you did in the past. Live in the moment like there's no tomorrow. Realize beauty in every moment, and appreciate things for what they are, good and bad.

Many are driving on the road with their head looking back instead of looking ahead. Others day-dream about their destination and in the process crash into a tree because they failed to pay attention when it's required — at the very moment.

And how do winners feel about the present? Winners are those people who in the midst of all their challenges (i.e. throughout the journey) realize they must face the present for what it is, and make the most of it. They don't dwell on the past nor escape into the future because they know that it's of no benefit to where they are and where they want to go.

Winners have their full attention and utmost energy in every given moment that they live in. It all happens in the present. Nothing in the past can be changed. A better future demands your complete attention to be on your present day.

Learn to accept and appreciate your life now. Your life is here, in the present.

Take a moment to reflect on this truth.
Consciously live this truth in week 42.

Winning Truth Number

43

Awareness

One pleasant afternoon, I was at the supermarket and without thinking, I got three chocolate bars, all of which I scoffed in a span of fifteen minutes. Later, I wondered to myself why I had committed such an act? After all there was nothing wrong with it, as it had been a long time since I had a chocolate bar. But it was not in line with my plan of losing weight to reach a lean and toned body.

I told my friend about my chocolate experience and in one statement he stunned me. He told me something so simple yet it rocked me to my core.

He said, 'It looks like you have decided to gain weight and be fat!'

I had nothing to say, even though for a millisecond I was tempted to say, ' No I'm not'. But I couldn't say no, because I just devoured three chocolate bars. I knew I wanted to achieve my goal, but my action told a different story.

His statement simply reminded me of what I already knew. I guess I had to hear it from him to really have the message driven home. My action was in conflict to my plan and the end result of achieving a lean and toned body (which was important to me).

To give in to temptation had a price to pay. To resist the temptation also had a price to pay. As always there is a price to pay and when aware, I would much rather pay the price to look good and feel good.

As a result of that experience, I'm continuously working on being aware in the moment, always asking myself 'Is my action helping in my path or is it making me go backwards'? I always know the answer and with that I follow through with my choice. Sometimes I feel like being naughty, and I indulge myself (hey you have to live and enjoy life, there is no point being miserable), but mostly I do things in line with the end result I desire.

Winners are constantly aware of their actions in order to make choices that are in line with their goals.

You must become aware of your actions. What are your actions really saying about you and your goals? Are they aligned with what you want? It's easy enough to change when you are aware of your actions and have a strong enough reason to do so. It's a choice you'll have to make.

You have no excuse when you choose and become aware.

Take a moment to reflect on this truth.
Consciously live this truth in week 43.

Winning Truth Number

44

A Winning Eye

Most people think winners have it easy. They see the end rewards winners enjoy and subconsciously come to conclusions like 'They're lucky', 'It's easy for them to say', 'They didn't go through what I went through', 'My situation is different'.

And here is the blatant truth.

It's not that winners have things easy in life, in fact, in many instances, it's the complete opposite. Winners go through more challenges than an average person. Winners choose to see challenges as a way to make them stronger and smarter, whilst the majority of people see it as the Great Wall of China in front of them.

Winners understand that they have a choice in how they decide to view events in their life. Winners leave their excuses at the door, because to them excuses are unacceptable. When the majority will give you 101 reasons as to why something can't be done, winners leave it all behind the door and go searching for solutions. They want to find a way in spite of the reasons given, rather than surrender to excuses.

Winners know a fundamental secret to winning and that's to have a winning eye. The difference between winners and the rest is their ability to see things differently. After all seeing it through the eyes of the majority will not help in their journey of wanting to move forward and excel.

When most people say 'I can't', winners ask, 'how can I?' and seek to find answers. Whether they find it in their lifetime or not, is not an issue, as long as they are on a path to find the answers. In their mind, they know that where there is a problem, there is bound to be a solution, period.

When the majority of people see the word 'impossible', winners actually see two words 'IM possible'.

When the majority of people reply as to whether a solution exists, you will hear something like, 'its NoWhere to be found'. A Winner would say, 'NowHere is where a solution will be found'.

It's all in how winners choose to see life, using their winning eye.

You have a winning eye. Choose to use it in your life.

Take a moment to reflect on this truth.
Consciously live this truth in week 44.

Winning Truth Number

45

In 25 Years, It Won't Matter

Just as I have, I know that you have come across events when you thought that it was the end of the world for you. That things couldn't get any worse, or there is no way you could cope with how tough life was (I recall breaking up with my first serious girlfriend felt that way to me at 20). Think of the time when you were preparing for exams in high school. It seemed like the biggest burden on your shoulders. I'm sure that today you would agree (and at times chuckle) as to how big you made it out to be, when it wasn't. What always amazes me is that over time, whatever seems to be a giant challenge is in most cases shrugged off lightly some years down the track.

Most people make a big deal out of small things. Many sweat the small stuff. Why? How could it possibly serve you in your quest to win? Winners always ask, 'Will this matter in the long run? Will it matter in 25 or 50 years time'? In most instances it won't. So whatever the challenge, they focus their eye on their prize. You will see these winners stand out as calm achievers. Always remind yourself about putting things in perspective, and remember that almost all challenges are diluted in their impact when you spread it over a long time span. You will realize no one giant challenge is and should ever be that troublesome.

You're well aware of this, because there are many experiences that you can look back on in your own life where you can easily see that nothing was ever as big a deal as it seemed in that moment. It never did and it never will.

When most people breakdown because of a challenge, winners breakthrough knowing that 'It's not that big a deal'.

You think you have challenges, speak to someone who hasn't had the pleasure of the basic things you have had so far in life. Think of all the people who went to bed last night and never got a chance to wake up this morning. I believe that this would be the biggest deal we all will ever face one day. If you're reading this today, it means you have been given an opportunity (please make the most of it). As long as you are breathing, as long as you are awake to face another day, then no challenge can and should ever be so big for you to remain consumed in.

Let things slide. Ask the smart questions. Put every challenge in perspective and push forward. That's how winners play the game. No one event will ever be the 'be all or end all'. It's never a big deal, so stop ever making it one.

Take a moment to reflect on this truth.
Consciously live this truth in week 45.

Winning Truth Number

46

Being Thankful

Thankful for what? You can be thankful for all the great things in your life, thankful for all the ordinary events, thankful for all the horrible events in your life. As hard as it will be if you are currently facing challenges, I will suggest that you must remain thankful for any event that takes place in your life. I want you to think about this.

How can you appreciate light if you haven't experienced darkness?

How can you appreciate the value of money if you haven't experienced the feeling of your pockets being dried up to the last cent?

How can you appreciate love, if you haven't experienced cruelty?

How can you appreciate equality, if you haven't experienced inequality?

How can you appreciate the good, if you haven't experienced the bad?

How can you appreciate happiness, if you haven't experienced sadness?

How can you appreciate a loved one, if you haven't experienced losing one?

How can you appreciate companionship, if you haven't experienced loneliness?

How can you appreciate trust, if you haven't experienced deceit?

How can you appreciate excitement, if you haven't experienced dullness?

How can you appreciate positivity, if you haven't experienced negativity?

I suggest that you start living life being thankful for what you are experiencing right now. Be thankful for all your struggles as it will make you a stronger person. Be thankful for the stress in your life for it will make you cherish the easygoing times. Be thankful for the challenges for it will bring you its set of opportunities. Be thankful for what your life has been so far, for it will give you the experience to be a better player today.

Winners know that every experience they face has a reason for it. Yes even the ones that tear them apart. They may not realize the reason in that moment, but when looked back some time later, they surely will. Winners are thankful for everything that has happened in their life. They are aware that the events in their life so far has shaped the person that they are today.

Be thankful before you go to sleep and be thankful when you wake up, after all, there is never a guarantee for another day. Live every day to the fullest. Combine this attitude with your ambition of growth and you will become an unstoppable force.

Think about everything you can be thankful for. I will suggest that there is plenty.

Take a moment to reflect on this truth. Consciously live this truth in week 46.

Winning Truth Number

47

Winning is Spelled COURAGE

Life is challenging and tough, I will be the first person to agree with you on that. Life will even be scary in many cases. On many occasions, winners are just as scared as the next person facing the same event. The one difference being that, winners will get over their fears by facing it head on. They will have the courage to step up and face a challenge, no matter what. It is the characteristic of every winner, to stand courageously and tall, even when they are most terrified.

In life, you are rewarded for the steps you take towards what you want, not wait for the best things to show up at your doorsteps. Getting out of your comfort zone as I mentioned earlier requires courage. You have to get the courage to rise and battle it out to get to the buffet of life in order to enjoy its offerings.

Winners would rather give something a go and fail but know that they gave it everything, rather than live life in regret. Have the courage to live like a first grade citizen that you are. Most people will never do so because they weren't courageous enough. There are no guarantees in life but there is a guarantee that if you give way to your fears and live life being a coward, you will be miserable.

At least, if you practice being courageous you will stand a great chance in getting everything you want. Just on the basis of 'Having no chance' vs. 'Having a chance', I would suggest that being courageous would be the only option for you to move forward if you want to be a winner.

Live life with your chin up. Be courageous to get out of your comfort zone. Be courageous to stand for something. Be courageous to take the risk. Be courageous to face your failures. Be courageous to live. Be courageous to dream. Be courageous to make your reality.

Think of a time when you faced a situation with courage. When was it? Where was it? How did it feel? Now, think of a time when you faced a situation without courage. How did that feel? You will always feel good when you have exhibited courage, even if you didn't get the desired result immediately.

Be very clear about the end result you want. Focus on the goals you have set out and nothing in between. Remember that what other people think of you is none of your business; it's their problem to keep. It's okay to fail, because it takes courage to make mistakes. Just get out and do it. Practice being patient and persistent remembering that every setback is getting you one step closer to your goal.

Most people are afraid of getting hurt, which is exactly what prevents them from trying. Remember that none of us will get out of life alive. Getting hurt is part of the game. So, be courageous and set forth on your journey to win.

Fortune does indeed favor the brave.

Take a moment to reflect on this truth.
Consciously live this truth in week 47.

Winning Truth Number

48

Required Ingredients

Winners are regularly faced with challenges. They understand that challenges are the required ingredients to win. In fact if you are not facing challenges, then the chances are you're operating well below your true capabilities. Some challenges arise as a result of poor choices you've made, whilst others are at times, out of your control. Nevertheless, you must learn to understand that a challenge, no matter how severe, is simply part of the game you have chosen to play. It's a required ingredient of the game.

What if you choose to resign and be at the complete mercy of the challenges you face?

Well, you won't stand a chance.

I would like to suggest that it's not the challenges that define you.

Winners are not shaped by the challenges they face, but by how they face their challenges. When faced with a challenge, you need to push through it, over it, or to the side of it. You do whatever you have to do, to get to the other side. As difficult as it may seem, or as hard as it may feel to recognize this fact, just like a coin, an event will always have two sides to it.

Take a large organization such as Google as an example. Do you think they let challenges hold them back? Do you think they bring everything to a complete halt because they are faced with a crisis? No, they continue to push forward, fine-tuning and working on their challenges along the way. It's important to note, that winners still keep their eyes locked on their vision. Therefore, they are constantly moving forward as opposed to many who are taking the sit and wait approach.

How you deal with challenges will determine whether you make the cut. It will determine whether you will rise and inherently, whether you'll win or not. For it's not what you are hit with, but how you deal with the hit. It's not how you are hit, but how hard you can hit back. It is not your size in the fight that matters, but size of the fight in you that will ultimately determine whether they will stand a chance at winning.

Welcome challenges in your world. Welcome challenges from your competition. The challenges you face will always help expand your thinking. It will help you grow stronger.

Take a moment to reflect on this truth. Consciously live this truth in week 48.

Winning Truth Number

49

BIG

If you are going to win, you might as well win big. If you are going to give something a go, you might as well give it a big shot. You must dream and you must imagine BIG. It's a must to being a winner.

You will spend the same amount of time and energy on whatever you choose to do, so make sure it's BIG

You have to think BIG

You have to attract BIG

You have to be BIG

You have to bring BIG

Most people think small because they are too afraid. They aren't afriad of failing, but possibly how BIG they can become, and the fear that they may not be capable kicks in. What they fail to realize is that throughout the process, they will grow to become the BIG person needed to make those BIG dreams a BIG reality.

The biggest partnerships happen with the biggest people. These people have the biggest minds. They have the biggest attitudes of making it happen. They bring their biggest thoughts to the table and together create the biggest results.

Like attracts like. If you want to attract big people to work with you and support you, then you need to be that BIG person first.

Are you thinking BIG? Are you being that BIG person? Be inspiring yourself and the people around you by thinking BIG, acting BIG and therefore being BIG.

BIG is scary, it's thrilling, it's filled with uncertainty and it will surely stretch you. Playing BIG will bring out the winner in you, because it does so with every winner.

What's stopping you from doing things BIG?

Just think of Richard Branson and the fun he is having. BIG is where all the fun is.

Take a moment to reflect on this truth. Consciously live this truth in week 49.

Winning Truth Number

50

We All Have Dislikes

I have had so many people tell me that they want to achieve great things in life. The only problem is that the tasks they have to accomplish to get there is something they dislike doing. I usually have two things to say.

(a) Too bad. If you really want something, then you will do whatever needs to be done to get there. Winning is simple. Nobody said it was easy.

(b) Reassess what you want. The chances are your goal is not something you really really really want. Because if it is, you will not put so much weight on the pain of the tasks but more so on the pleasure of the end reward.

I will suggest the same for you. Take your pick from the above two choices because winners dislike the tasks that you do too. They simply have more pleasure associated with their end reward than the pain of doing the tasks. They see themselves living their dreams and reaching their goals. Everything else in between is simply a process. It's just something they have to do.

I remember talking with a friend who was training for the Olympics. He would get up at 5 a.m. and go running in the cold weather as part of his preparation to ensure he was extremely fit for the big day. I asked him how he got himself out of bed in the cold morning and go running with such ease?

What he said has stayed with me as a great reminder whenever I am staring down the barrel of challenges I face to get to any of my goals. He said, 'Kevin, you are not alone. I love my sleep just as much as you do, and a few years back, you would have never seen me get up before 5 a.m. But my dream is to get to the Olympics and I will do whatever I need to do to get there. When I hear the alarm at 4:50 a.m., I don't hear an annoying noise. I hear that I am another day closer to living my dream. That's how I get out of bed without thinking twice about it.'

Understand that all good things require work, just as implementing these truths that you are reading for your life. You are not alone. Winners love to do what you do and dislike the tasks you dislike too. But if there is a goal to achieve within a time frame, they will do whatever it takes to get there. Winners practice and develop a much higher association of pleasure to achieving their goals compared to the pain of doing the tasks.

They have learned to pick things that ignite them so that they can go through the tasks they dislike along the way. Find something that will *ignite* you.

**Take a moment to reflect on this truth.
Consciously live this truth in week 50.**

Winning Truth Number

51

Regular Check Ups

A common misconception many have is mentors and coaches are only for those who are not successful. The truth is everybody needs to have someone to hold him or her accountable for their actions. Winners know this more than anyone and truly value the importance of having someone keep them in check. In fact the better they get, the more they see the need for it to avoid the risk of becoming complacent and caught up in their own success by way of their ego (which has brought many down, including myself in the past).

A question I am asked often is 'Why would anyone need a coach if they are already doing well? That's a great question and my response is a simple one, 'The best soccer teams in the world still have coaches'. You don't see top teams, athletes or individuals without coaches. Think of Manchester United, Tiger Woods and Shahrukh Khan. All Winners in their own right and all have coaches.

Having a coach is not about necessarily being at the bottom in your life results. It's about being able to further enhance your performance to win. It is about pushing that envelope, about constantly bringing out the best in you on occasions when it's tough for you to do so.

Every Winner has a coach. A coach is not a friend, although he could be one. Generally, a friend is one who will tell you why its okay if you haven't achieved what you said you would. A coach is someone who will hold you accountable when the majority are too worried about hurting your feelings.

Winners always have someone to tell them *how it is*. They are told the truth without the sugar coat. A coach holds you accountable and doesn't take any bulls@$# you try to spin their way.

Whether you are in sports, business or simply on a personal level (the most important of all) you must get yourself a coach to hold you accountable for your actions. Whether it is someone you respect and has the time to do so, hiring a personal coach, creating a mastermind group or joining a like minded circle, it is a must for every winner.

Whatever you do, get yourself a coach, someone who can help bring out the best in you because remember, winning is the sum of your habits and they will keep you in check. Ideally, depending on what you are looking for, you must find a coach or mentor who has achieved what you want to achieve. A coach that can tell you how it is, although cruel at times, is the truest friend one could be because your coach will have your best interest at heart.

At the end of it all your focus should be on your results. Get all the help you can get.

Take a moment to reflect on this truth. Consciously live this truth in week 51.

Winning Truth Number

52

A Box Office Hit

All winners have asked this question, the response of which resulted in them taking the actions they felt was right for them. *How do I want the movie that will be my life played back to me on my last day?* Why would you do something you don't like, and then look back on your last day of life regretting what you have done? What's the point of looking back and saying, 'I didn't live a full life'? Is that how you would want it to be?

Let's fast forward to the last day of your life. You are 101 years old (or longer), and you have one last day to watch a movie which will be a reflection of your life journey. What will this life journey of yours look like? Will it be dull, boring, complacent, living within assumed safety nets that never existed, or will it be filled with excitement, joy, laughter and plenty of learned lessons from giving life a good go?

Will your movie be filled with numerous 'What ifs?' Will it be filled with regret? Sadness for things you never tried? Grief for things you didn't say and do? Will it be filled with sorrow because now that you're reflecting at 101 years old, all the big things you thought mattered really didn't? People never cared about you when you thought they did (they were too worried about themselves and what you thought of them). You could have done more and didn't. You could have lived more but didn't. You could have loved more but didn't. You could have lived in the moment and enjoyed but you didn't.

Will you reflect on the times that you didn't have the skills to do something but plunged into it anyway because you were determined enough to learn as you go? Will you reflect on the time that you were brave enough to fail? Will you reflect on the love you had in life for the people around you, for nature, and for the appreciation you gave every moment?

You own the first day of your life, you own the last, and you own everything in between.

Look at different parts of your life and ask yourself what would make for an exciting story to reflect on? That's what a winner would do. You have the first and last say in it. This is your life. This is your privilege, your birthright. Make it happen, make it count. Stand for something. Strive for something. Create an amazing story that will be your life, one that you will enjoy when you reflect back on your last day on this planet.

On the last day, all you can do is reflect. Today, however, you have the ability to *create* that reflection. You have come to the end of this book but your winning journey continues beyond these pages. What you do with your life is your choice. All I can say is make it a Box Office Hit.

Take a moment to reflect on this truth. Consciously live this truth in week 52.

Author's Last Comment

Congratulations on having gone through this book.

Remember the Power between the pages you have gone through.

Read and re-read each chapter, more importantly take it in and apply it.

Now that you are aware of these truths, the workload is on you.

You are ahead of 99% of the population that don't know and sadly will live life unaware of Why Winners Win. You can't use that excuse any more, so take what you have learned and live it.

There is a winner within every one of us, and there is one in you.

Practice each truth daily until it becomes you.

I would like to hear about your winning stories personally, so keep in touch by emailing your story and testimonial to info@KevinAbdulrahman.com.

My vision is to reach over 1 billion people, and to know that I helped make a positive difference in your life is the reason why I do what I do.

Here's to you Winning Everyday

In friendship

Kevin Abdul1rahman
'The Man Inspiring Millions'

Stay in Touch

We want to hear your winning breakthroughs and success stories.

Stay in touch and let us know how you are doing. You can do so by going on www.thisisTHEBOOK.com.

We are in the process of compiling several books—one of which will be a compilation of people achieving great success in any aspect of their lives. If you would like to be considered to have a chapter in The Book on today's success stories (title to be confirmed) then do submit it www.thisisTHEBOOK.com.

Ensure you give us all your details correctly so we can contact you should you qualify.

Bulk Purchases for Your TEAM

The Book on *Whatever You're Into* has been translated into many languages and many Organizations stack it as a Must Have and Must Read Book to help individuals

a. Develop a Winning Mind

b. Accelerate, Achieve and Surpass their Targets

c. Become Empowered and Motivated

d. Enhance Ownership and Accountability

e. Boost Personal Effectiveness

e. Create Leadership From Within

If you would like associates, friends, family and your fellow team members to achieve all of the above and more, *then contact our team to see how* we can help you to be a winner.

Email us: info@KevinAbdulrahman.com. We will be happy to help.

To Reach the Author

Media inquiries:

For all media inquiries, publicity photos, interview questions, or article syndication and reprint rights, please forward your request: media@KevinAbdulrahman.com

General inquiries:

For all general inquiries and how you can have Kevin Abdulrahman speak to your group, please make your request: info@KevinAbdulrahman.com

Ten Reasons to Have Kevin Abdulrahman (The Man Inspiring Millions) at your Next Event

√ Attendees of Kevin Abdulrahman's Talk regularly vote him as The Best Motivational Speaker across Asia, Middle East and the Indian Subcontinent – He is one of the most sought after speakers in the region.

√ Kevin Abdulrahman inspires the people to be the Driving Force of Today and the Powerhouse of Tomorrow.

√ Kevin Abdulrahman is a Speaker who connects with his audience.

√ He designs and delivers his message with impact. He is informative and inspiring.

√ Kevin Abdulrahman is known to be an Easy Speaker to work with. He takes pride in taking on a partnership role with any organizer ensuring a Winning Result.

√ Kevin Abdulrahman is committed to this Region and is always open to discussing more than just a one-off talk.

√ Kevin Abdulrahman always seeks to create a winning and lasting impact beyond a requested Keynote Speech. This is done through book deals made available for your audience as take home gifts for a lasting impact.

√ Kevin Abdulrahman will happily contribute articles to your local newspaper/magazine/in-house newsletters

√ Kevin Abdulrahman will happily go on air to help promote the event for you and with you.

√ Kevin Abdulrahman has a vision of wanting to help one billion people Get Inspired, Get Informed and Get Going!!! By having him in front of your audience, you are contributing towards a vision to make the world a better place.

About the Author

Please take a moment and go on to Google.

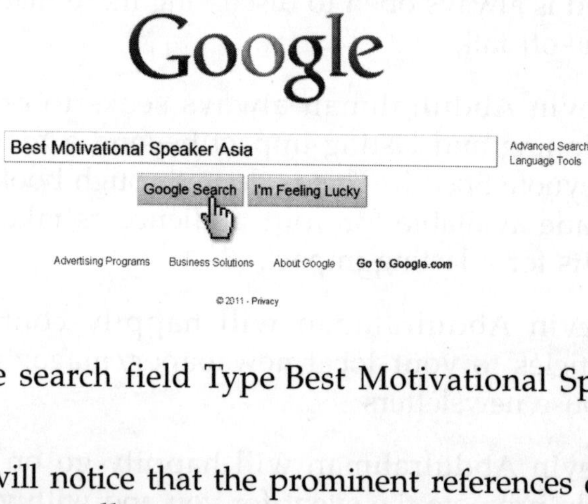

In the search field Type Best Motivational Speaker Asia

You will notice that the prominent references on the front page all point to the work of one Man-Kevin Abdulrahman.

Globally known as The Man Inspiring Millions, Kevin Abdulrahman's message is connecting in a big way in the Middle East, Asia and Indian Subcontinent.

On an International Level, he makes for only a handful of sought after speakers who has the edge of

Youth coupled with the experience of having spoken and continues to speak across Five Continents.

Kevin Abdulrahman believes in a simple philosophy – *"The Quality of Your Results is a Direct Reflection of the Quality of Your Mind"*. In your team, group or an organizational environment, the Quality of Your Results is the Direct Reflection of the Quality of the Collective Minds in Your Group.

As a Speaker of substance who delivers every time, Kevin Abdulrahman has been voted by his Seminar/ Conference attendees, students and raving fans as the Best Motivational, Inspirational and Leadership Speaker in Asia, Middle East and the Indian Sub continent.

Book Kevin Abdulrahman, 'The Man Inspiring Millions'

Today, the name Kevin Abdulrahman is synonymous with being one of the most Recognised, Renowned, Requested, Respected and Relevant Motivational Speakers of Our Time.

With an extensive client list, Kevin Abdulrahman is Frequently Booked and Flown around the world to Consult, Coach, Counsel, Speak to, Train and Work with Athletes, Celebrities, CEOs, Executives, Government Entities, Models, Musicians, NGOs, Private Companies, Public Organizations, Royalties, Schools, Sports Teams, Universities and everyone in between, helping them Raise Their Performance to The Next Level.

Kevin Abdulrahman Empowers, Engages and Evokes Emotions from his audience for them to reflect on the importance of where they are, where they want to go in life, what decisions they must make, and what actions they have to take.

When your fellow Industry Colleagues are looking for a Motivational, Inspirational and Leadership Speaker to deliver, they call for Kevin Abdulrahman – The Man that is relied upon to get the job done Every Time!!!

Your Audience Deserve The Best.

Give them The Best

Give them The Man Inspiring Millions

Give them Kevin Abdulrahman

Book Kevin Abdulrahman, The Best Motivational Speaker in Asia to Help You, Your People, Your Groups, Your Team, and Your Organizations Get Inspired, Get Informed and Get Going!!!

Contact the Management Team on
Info@KevinAbdulrahman.com